THE KIDS' BOOK OF CARDS AND POSTERS

BY MATTHEW BARISH

illustrated by Erika Wallace and others

Prentice-Hall, Inc., Englewood Cliffs, New Jersey

The author would like to thank the children and teachers at the Little Red Schoolhouse in New York City, especially Marcia Wallace, for their cooperation on this book.

Copyright © 1973 by Matthew Barish

All rights reserved. No part of this book may be reproduced in any form or by any means, except for the inclusion of brief quotations in a review, without permission in writing from the publisher.

Printed in the United States of America *J

Prentice-Hall International, Inc., London
Prentice-Hall of Australia, Pty. Ltd., North Sydney
Prentice-Hall of Canada, Ltd., Toronto
Prentice-Hall of India Private Ltd., New Delhi
Prentice-Hall of Japan, Inc., Tokyo

Library of Congress Cataloging in Publication Data

Barish, Matthew.
The kids' book of cards and posters.

SUMMARY: Lists appropriate holidays and occasions throughout the year for greeting cards and posters and discusses the necessary materials and techniques for creating them.
Bibliography: p.
1. Greeting cards—Juvenile literature.
2. Posters—Juvenile literature. [1. Greeting cards.
2. Posters] I. Wallace, Erika, illus. II. Title.
TT872.B37   760   72-13859
ISBN 0-13-515114-7
0-13-515098-1 (pbk.)

10 9 8 7 6 5 4 3

INTRODUCTION: HOW TO USE THIS BOOK

This is a book about how to create your own cards and posters. Cards are a way of using words and pictures to communicate with someone you know, while posters are a way of attracting the attention of people you may not know. A card is meant to be looked at closely, for a long time; a poster is designed to catch the public's eye and to get your message across in a split second.

The same techniques are used to make both cards and posters, though. Some of the techniques in this book are good for making many cards (for invitations or Christmas cards) or posters (to announce a play all over town) and others are good for making one card (like a special Valentine) or one fancy poster (like a birthday poster for a friend). You can use these techniques by yourself, or in a group.

Chapter II is a good place to start: it contains many ideas for making cards and posters. You can take off from there and develop other ideas from the historical techniques discussed in Chapter I.

If after you have looked over Chapter III, you want to learn more about a certain technique, you can check the list of books in the back of this one for specialized help. And if you have trouble finding supplies in your town, you can find out where to buy materials by mail.

When you've had a chance to make a lot of cards and posters, Chapter V is a good place to find out how to make money from your ideas. And even if you don't think your cards and posters are good enough to sell, you can be sure that the people who look at them and receive them in the mail will love them because you made them.

CONTENTS

INTRODUCTION:
HOW TO USE THIS BOOK / iii
I—A LITTLE BIT OF HISTORY / 7
II—LOVE IS THE MESSAGE / 11
III—BEFORE YOU BEGIN / 42
IV—HOW TO DO IT: ONE AT A TIME / 49
V—HOW TO DO IT: MULTIPLES / 77
VI—THAT EXTRA BONUS / 85
VII—MAILING CARDS
AND POSTING POSTERS / 87
VIII—WHERE TO FIND SUPPLIES / 90
BIBLIOGRAPHY / 93
INDEX / 95

I
A LITTLE BIT OF HISTORY

Communicating through words and pictures is an ancient tradition. People have known for a long time that pictures can tell a story and that words can be pleasing to the eye as well as the ear.

Nobody knows who made the first greeting card or the first illustrated poster. Greeting cards have their origins in notes sent with presents, in stamped coins and tokens, and in decorated letters. Posters began as simple announcements of plays and signs for shops, extensions of *graffiti*.

The first cards and posters were decorated with woodcuts. The first modern greeting card was printed about the time of the Gutenberg Bible, in the fifteenth century. Posters were hand-made or printed in small quantities and more common, and less elegant, since

their main purpose was to attract attention to some event or product, not a personal greeting.

The invention of lithography in the nineteenth century created a boom in the number of greeting cards and posters. Cards were usually printed in black, and then colored by hand. Most posters were very plain. When color lithography was introduced in Europe, and it became possible to reproduce paintings in large quantities, looking very much like the originals, great artists like Toulouse-Lautrec and Kate Greenaway began to create lovely posters and cards for wide distribution.

Louis Prang brought fine color lithography to the United States, and produced many beautiful—and very expensive—greeting cards. His cards were put together by hand, and included padding, silk and satin ribbons, and fancy lettering. Prang employed the finest artists to do illustrations for his cards.

The first posters of real artistic merit were made in France in the 1830's. Some of these posters were advertisements for products, others were announcements of plays, and still others were masterpieces created for no particular purpose. Toulouse-Lautrec in France and Aubrey Beardsley in England perfected poster art in Europe.

The fine French posters announcing actress Sarah Bernhardt's appearances inspired great enthusiasm in America in the 1890s. Advertisers noticed how people reacted to the posters, and commissioned their own posters to advertise their products. It was not long before American poster art was outstanding. Maxfield Parrish, Ben Shahn and Roy Lichtenstein are among the great American poster artists.

Today both posters and greeting cards are big business. Every movie is announced with an eye-catching poster, and about eight billion greeting cards are sold every year. Printing techniques have improved so that the cards and posters are more beautiful than ever, and they are produced in large enough quantities so that they need not be expensive.

II
LOVE IS THE MESSAGE

Greeting cards are for all occasions—and any occasion. The message can be aimed at a special occasion or it can be simply a pretty way of saying "I'm thinking of you." Posters too can be for no occasion or any occasion; or they can announce a special event. In this chapter there are suggestions for occasions for making cards and posters, but they are only suggestions. The best occasions for making cards and posters are up to you, and the people you make them for.

JANUARY

News Year's Day used to be the most important holiday of the year. The Egyptians and the Romans celebrated the coming of the new year in the spring, and exchanged gifts and tokens at that time. The first greeting cards in Europe were sent at the beginning of the New Year. You can surprise your friends by sending New Year's cards as well as Christmas cards, or instead of Christmas cards. If someone you forgot sends you a Christmas card, you can send him a New Year card.

Get well Cards are always welcome when your friends or relatives get sick. Since being sick is so boring, it's not a bad idea to send a card every day. A card that is funny cheers up a person who's in bed, and sometimes you can send a pretty card with a message (all the latest news) inside.

Snow safety Posters are a good way to remind yourself and your classmates to be careful when you are sledding, skating or snowmobiling. You can list the many rules of snow safety, or concentrate one poster on one aspect of snow safety.

FEBRUARY

Groundhog's Day is February 2, and it's a nice way to say hello to friends or relatives who are far away. A simple picture of the groundhog seeing his shadow is appropriate with a personal message inside that will cheer up your friends during the dreary winter months.

Valentine's Day, February 14, is an important occasion for sending cards. You will want to send all kinds of Valentines: to your friends, who will enjoy a funny one; to your relatives, who might prefer sweet ones, and to people you like best of all, who deserve a fancy Valentine, perhaps a collage card.

Class elections call for a poster featuring yourself, explaining why you should be a class officer. It can be funny or serious, depending on your taste. A picture of yourself, a list of your good qualities or what you will do for the class should be on the poster.

Team Recruitment Posters arouse interest in sports among your friends and schoolmates. Whether you want to start a bicycle racing team, a baseball team, or a bowling team, you will want to announce it. We are looking for kids who love to play baseball—try-outs are on Saturday morning, etc. Photos of the present team, drawings of kids participating in the sport, or just a picture of a bat or a diving board will get people to notice your poster.

MARCH

For your *class play*, you can make a poster announcing it, the way people do for movies and Broadway shows. The poster should tell what the play is about, when and where it is to be held, and who's in it. If you charge admission, you can tell how much it will cost. The most important part of the poster is the picture that shows the mood of the play. You can show a close-up of one of the leading characters, or you can show a scene from the play.

Individual programs can be made using stencil or printing techniques. The program for everyone in the audience is like a card, with information about the play. If you like, you can include nice comments from people who have seen the play. If you are having a lot of people at the play, you might want to xerox or mimeograph the words, and have each person in the class decorate the programs for a personal touch.

St. Patrick is Ireland's patron saint, and his birthday, March 17, is celebrated wherever Irish people have settled. St. Patrick's Day is a light-hearted holiday, celebrated with parades and parties. Your card might feature a shamrock, a shillelagh or a leprechaun. And remember, the color for the day is green.

APRIL

Easter and Passover are two religious festivals that fall in the spring. Traditional Easter symbols are the cross, the Easter lily, rabbits carrying baskets of eggs and candy and new Easter outfits. Passover is a religious occasion when Jewish families get together for the Seder, commemorating the flight of the Jews from Egypt. Family scenes, a glass of wine and unleavened bread (matzohs) are just right for Passover cards.

Lost Pet Posters can help you recover lost pets. You can put posters around your neighborhood telling what your pet looks like, what his name is, where he lives and your phone number. A photograph or drawing of your pet should be included on each poster.

Friendship Cards are one way to say "hello" to friends. Sometimes you think of a friend who has moved away, or a cousin you see only once a year, or a pal from camp. You don't have anything important to say except "I'm thinking of you." This is the time to send a friendship card. It can say simply, "Hello!" or "I miss you," or you can write a letter on the inside.

A *Register Your Bike Poster* makes sense now that spring is here. You can make a poster telling your friends and classmates where and when to register their bikes with the police, so that if the bike is lost or stolen they can help you find it. A big picture of a bike catches people's eyes, and a few words about why a kid should take the time to register his bike is important.

MAY

Parade Posters tell people where and when to come, and show them why they should want to come. For a patrol parade, for instance, you might say, "We've been practicing all year—Come see us at our best."

Mother's Day Cards can express your feelings for your mother with a pretty picture and a personal message. Even though you see your mother every day, she will love to be remembered on Mother's Day. In a way this is an easy card to make because you know your mother pretty well, and you know she'll like whatever you do.

Confirmation and Graduation Cards are a way of saying "I'm proud of you" to a friend or relative. For Catholics and many Protestants, Confirmation usually takes place when a person is 12. For many Jews, the Bar Mitzvah (for boys) and the Bas Mitzvah (for girls) takes place when a person is 13. In Reform temples, Confirmation takes place when the person is 16. You can decorate your cards with the Star of David, the Torah, candles, or the Bible.

Graduation is always a big event, from nursery school through medical school. A humorous card is appropriate for this happy occasion, or you can feature a diploma, a mortarboard or a cheerful bouquet.

JUNE

Engagements, Weddings and Anniversaries are happy occasions for cards. If you have friends or relatives who are recently engaged or married, you can send them a cheerful card congratulating them. Rings, flowers, lovebirds and hearts are all just right for these cards.

Even if you see your parents every day, they will be pleased if you remember their anniversary. You can make a drawing of what their wedding looked like, or include a photograph from their honeymoon on their card. Different anniversaries have different symbols: gold for the fiftieth anniversary, silver for the twenty-fifth, paper for the first anniversary. A design around the number for the years they've been married is also a good idea.

Father's Day falls on the third Sunday in June. It's a chance to remind your father that you like him, and appreciate what he's done for you. You can make a card with a map, suggesting that maybe someday you will go there together. A photograph or a drawing of your father doing something with you also makes a good Father's Day card.

No Litter Posters remind people how easy it is to

care a "litter" bit. In the summer when you have time to enjoy sports and travel, you realize how important not littering and not polluting is. You can make a poster to hang in your neighborhood, showing a photograph of how ugly litter is. You might want to have a litterbug on your poster as well.

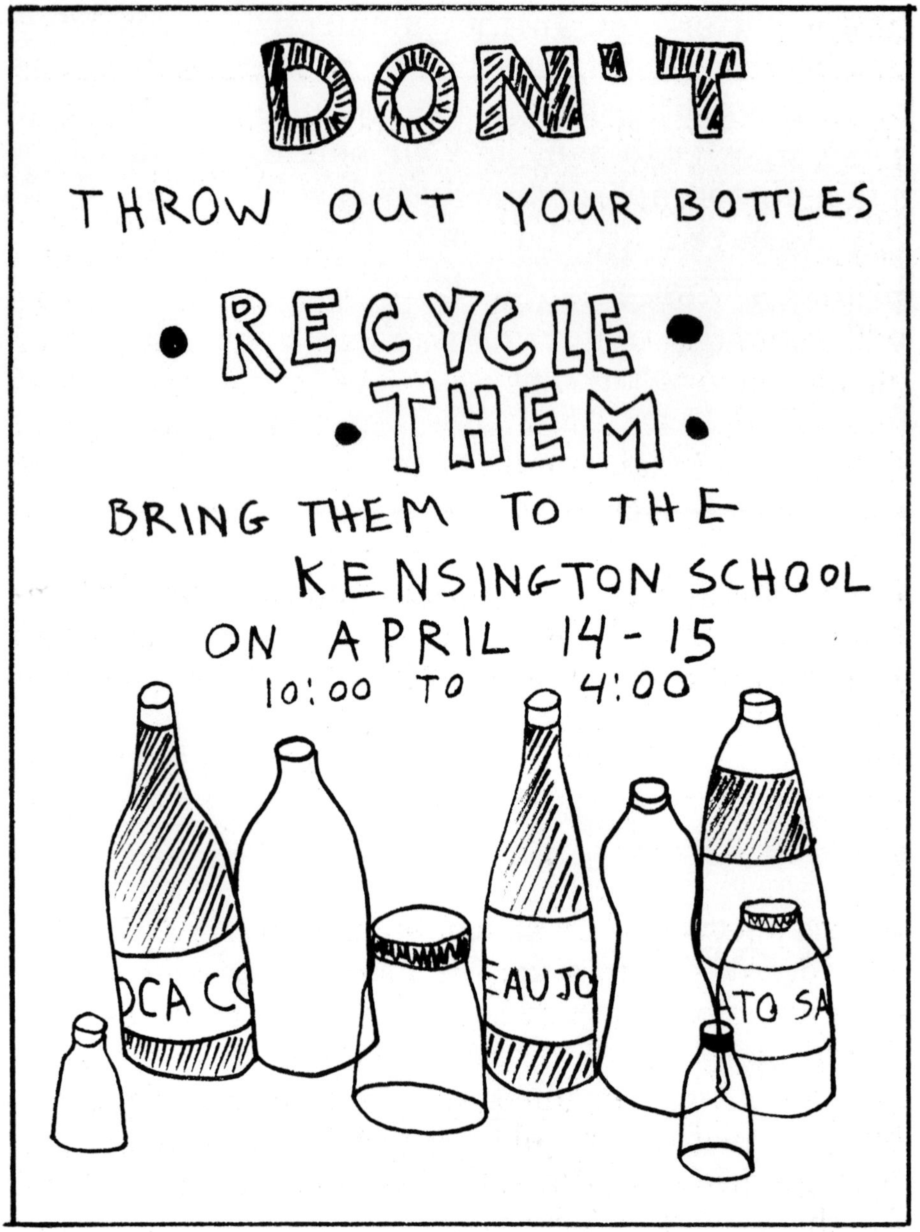
DON'T
THROW OUT YOUR BOTTLES
RECYCLE
THEM
BRING THEM TO THE
KENSINGTON SCHOOL
ON APRIL 14 - 15
10:00 TO 4:00
OCA CO
EAUJO
ATO SA

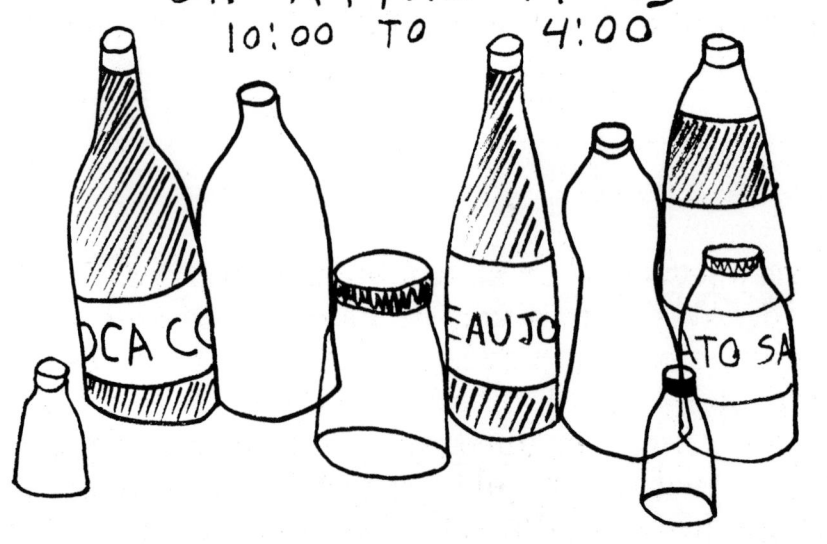

JULY

Recycling Posters remind your friends and neighbors to bring their bottles, aluminum cans and newspapers to the center that you have set up with your scout troop or neighborhood association. A catchy picture of kids bringing in newspapers and things will remind people that *they* can help. The poster should include what times the center is open, what you will do with the money you make from it, and how the materials should be prepared. Little pictures can make this clearer.

Lemonade or Kool-Aid Stand Posters bring customers to your stand. One block away from your stand you can put a sign that says "Thirsty? Turn on Deal Street for Cool Refreshment." Then you can have a big sign by your stand that explains that your lemonade is organic, or that your kool-aid comes in eight different flavors.

A new apartment or new home is a fine occasion for a card. We live in a very mobile society and we are constantly on the move. Parents get new jobs. The family gets larger or richer and moves to bigger quarters. You can illustrate someone waving goodbye, or picture the old or new house on your card. A large drawing of a set of keys is a fitting symbol for the move to a new home.

AUGUST

Congratulations Cards are always fun to receive. When you win second prize in the science fair, or the dentist takes your braces off, or your mother finally lets you buy a dog, you feel very proud and happy. The small things that happen to friends and relatives, from having a new baby in the family, to retirement, to getting into college are very important to *them*, and they'll be delighted if you remember them with a congratulations card.

Parks Program Posters bring kids together to explore the woods. In many areas, nature centers and the recreation department sponsor hikes and nature study programs. A picture of a chipmunk or some animal that you saw on one of the hikes, or a drawing of kids hiking through the woods might be interesting.

Bon Voyage cards send your friends off to a good start wishing them a wonderful time. A shipping tag tied to a trunk saying "Any room for me?" is funny. A map of the proposed trip folded up to card size with a message inside printed in bright colors is a fine send-off.

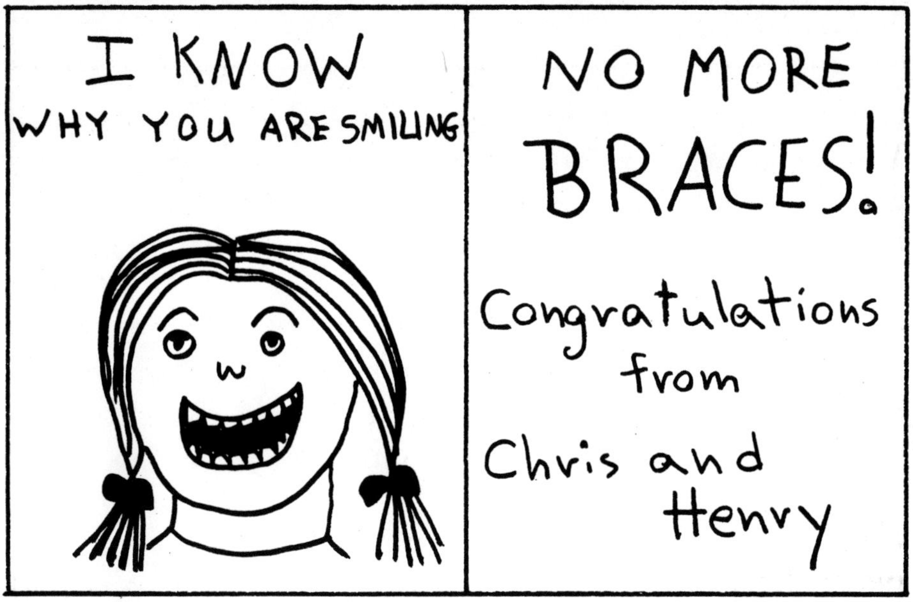
I KNOW
WHY YOU ARE SMILING
NO MORE
BRACES!
Congratulations
from
Chris and
Henry

CONGRATULATIONS
MOM
NO
SMOKING
CIGARETTES

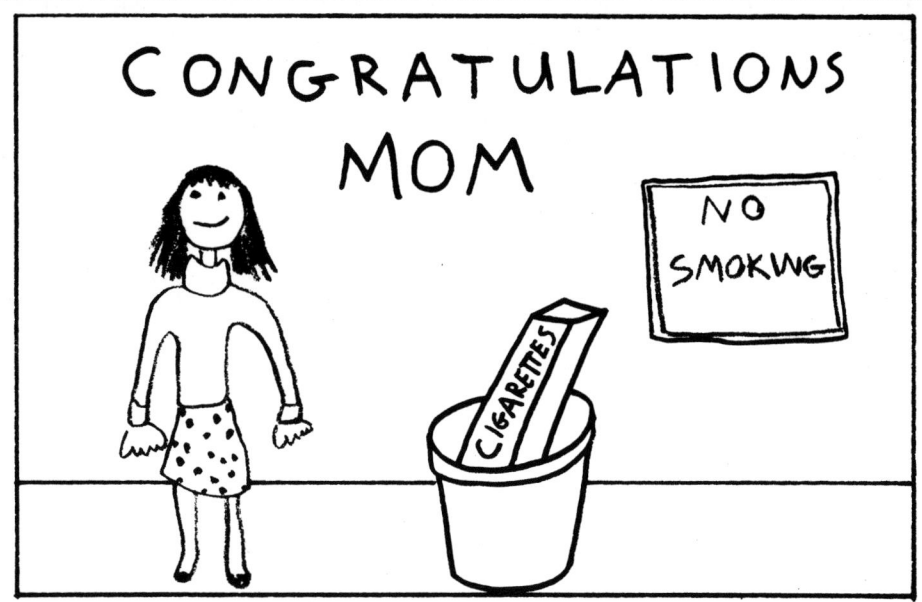

SEPTEMBER

Hebrew New Year (Rosh Hashanah) falls between September 5 and October 6. Ten days later is the holiday, Yom Kippur, the holiest day of the year. This is a religious time for Jews. All cards you send should have religious symbols, such as the star of David, a scroll, a branched candelabra, a synagogue and scenes of Israel. You might want to simply write "Shalom," the Hebrew word for peace or The Ten Commandments on the front of the card. A traditional greeting is "May you be inscribed in the Book of Life," which comes from a prayer book.

Scout Meeting Announcements make good posters. If you are starting a scout troop or a camera club, and you'd like other kids to join, you can make a poster urging new members to come to your meeting. The time and place should be on the poster, and a picture showing the club's activities.

Nutrition Posters remind us to eat better to live better. A picture of a happy kid eating breakfast, or a picture of the four basic food groups makes a good poster for the classroom. If someone in your family is dieting, you might make a cheerful poster for the refrigerator door—"We know you can do it, Mom" or if you are the one who's dieting, you could make a poster to remind yourself, like "Do I really want to eat?"

OCTOBER

Halloween Cards can feature many symbols, including ghosts, witches and devils. You might draw a picture of children trick-or-treating in costume, or bobbing for apples at a Halloween party. The jack-o-lantern, a traditional symbol of Halloween, is also a good choice for a Halloween card.

Tooth Posters remind us how important it is to care for our teeth. Everyone hates to go to the dentist, but it's something we all have to do. You can make posters for your class, showing a big toothy smile, reminding you to go to the dentist, brush your teeth and eat right for healthy teeth. Your dentist might like such a poster for his office too.

Bake Sales can be more successful with posters. Poster paints are good for making a chocolate cake look mouth-watering, or you can draw pictures of pies and cookies with crayon that will make people eager to come to the bake sale. Be sure to tell when and where the bake sale is, and who's sponsoring it.

Columbus Day Cards are big surprises. Who would think of sending a card on Columbus Day? Not many people, but if you send one, people will be pleased and surprised. You can show the three ships, the *Nina*, the *Pinta* and the *Santa Maria*, or Columbus talking with the Indians or spying land for the first time. You can also include a silly rhyme inside to cheer people up.

NOVEMBER

Thanksgiving Cards commemorate the harvest feast, held in 1621, a year after the Pilgrims settled at Plymouth, Massachusetts. When Abraham Lincoln was president, he proclaimed the day a national holiday. Since it is a harvest celebration featuring native American foods, you may be thinking of pictures of turkeys, ears of corn, and sheaves of wheat. Or you might prefer to draw the Pilgrims and the Indians sharing the first Thanksgiving.

Book Fair Posters tell kids in your neighborhood and at your school where and when the fair takes place. You can make up a slogan like, "Take a look and buy a book" or "Books are a new world," or "Explore the world of books at the school book fair." You can sometimes get a few book jackets to use on your posters, or you can draw a funny picture of kids surrounded by books.

Sympathy Cards are always appreciated. Sometimes people you know die. You want to comfort their friends and family but it is hard to think of things to say at this time. A sympathy card can be a lovely picture and a simple note, like "I'm sorry" or "I'm thinking of you."

DECEMBER

Christmas, the anniversary of Christ's birth, has become a social holiday with the idea of "peace on earth, good will towards men" behind it. If you want to make religious cards you might think about the three wise men, Mary and the baby Jesus, or the star of Bethlehem. If you choose a secular theme, Santa Claus and his reindeer, holly and ivy, carol singers, Christmas trees and snow might go well on your card. Since Christmas is a time for families to get together, you might want to take a picture of your family or pets with the Christmas tree or with Santa Claus.

34

At *Hanukkah* time, Jews celebrate the rededication of the Temple in Jerusalem which the Israelites recaptured from the Syrians in 195 B.C. When the lamp in the Temple was lighted, there was only enough oil in it to burn one day, but it miraculously continued to burn for eight days. During Hanukkah, the eight candles of the Menorah are lighted one by one, over the eight day period in remembrance of this joyous victory. Symbols for this festive holiday include the Menorah, the Dreidel (a top decorated with Hebrew letters), and happy family scenes.

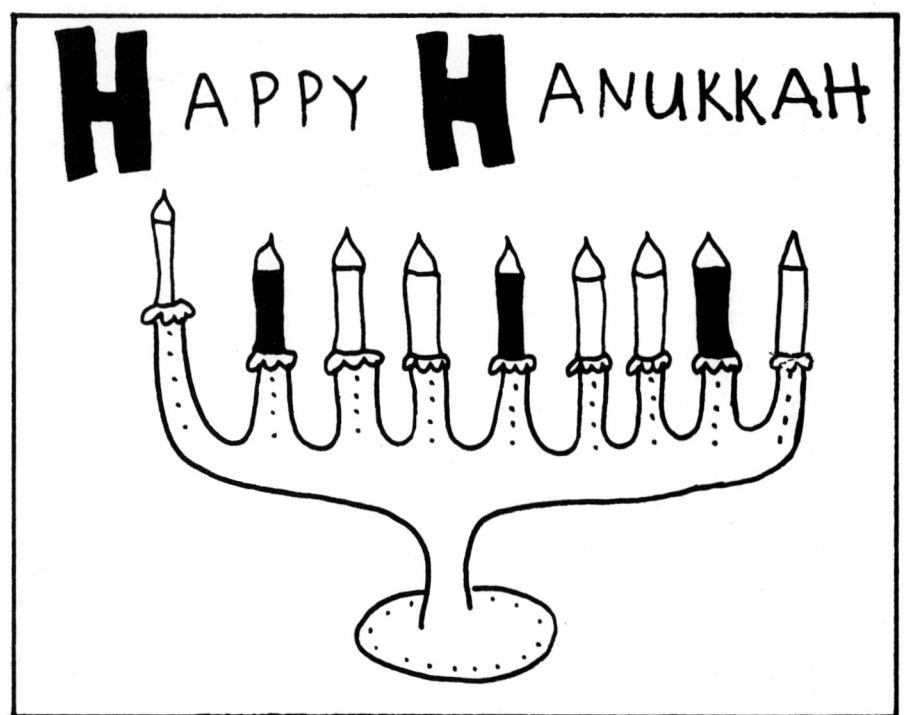

Charity Posters remind us how we can help others. At Christmas, when we are thinking of all the presents we'll be getting, we sometimes forget about people who have nothing. Many schools sponsor drives for money, food or presents to help people whose Christmas doesn't look like much fun. The poster should be cheerful, but not humorous. "You can help" is the message you want to impress upon people who see the poster.

Birthday Cards are always appreciated by the person who receives them. Everybody's favorite holiday is his birthday. You can brighten up your friends' birthdays with cards made especially for them. A picture of your friend or a photograph of the two of you together is a good start for a card. If you want to use a design on your card, you might use the number of the birthday as a theme. Balloons, birthday cakes, favors and big stacks of presents also make attractive subjects for birthday cards.

Thank You Cards are easy to make, and they assure the giver that you liked his present and that it got to you safely. A picture of you and the present on the front, or a simple grinning face convey your happiness. Thank you notes written on cards with a pretty design are also welcome when you have eaten dinner at a friend's house, or spent the night. Some people make a lot of cards with a simple design on them, using a stencil or printing technique, and write a personal note inside when it's time to say "thank you."

Invitations to parties can make people excited about the event, and give them a record of when and where the party is to be, so they won't forget. Your invitations can feature a picture of the person you're inviting, a picture of your dog, or a scene with balloons and cake—anything that is personal and fun. Be sure to mention where the party is (you can include a map), and the time (you can draw a picture of a clock) so your guests won't forget.

Birthday posters are cards that last forever. You can make a birthday poster for new babies you know, welcoming them to the world. You can also make birthday posters for your family and friends, showing pictures of things that they'd like to look at every day—your father in that sports car he hopes to buy some day, a picture of your best friend and his dog camping out together, or a picture of a new baby's family. Birthday posters can also show bright designs and a simple message.

III
BEFORE YOU BEGIN

Once you have decided to make a poster or greeting card, what do you do? You know what the occasion is, but how shall you treat it—in a funny way, in a serious way, or in a lovely way? Think about the people who will look at the card or poster, and decide which way they'd prefer. Now you're ready to try out several ideas for your card or poster.

MAKING A DUMMY

you need: scratch paper, pencil with a good eraser, scissors.

A dummy is a rough sketch of what you want your card to look like. A greeting card and poster both have three elements: the art, the lettering and your logo. On a greeting card, the title and the art usually go on the front of the card, the message inside, and your trademark on the back. On a poster, all three elements have to go on the front, with the lettering more outstanding than it would be on a card.

43

When you make a dummy, sketch various arrangements of art and lettering to see which is the most effective. If you can't decide which rough sketch you like best, ask a friend or your father which looks best to him.

A dummy will let you see what your card will look like without the color and finishing touches. Check to make sure that your lettering is well-spaced, that your margins are wide enough, and that the art and the lettering go together.

Now you are ready to decide which technique will work best for the card or poster you have in mind.

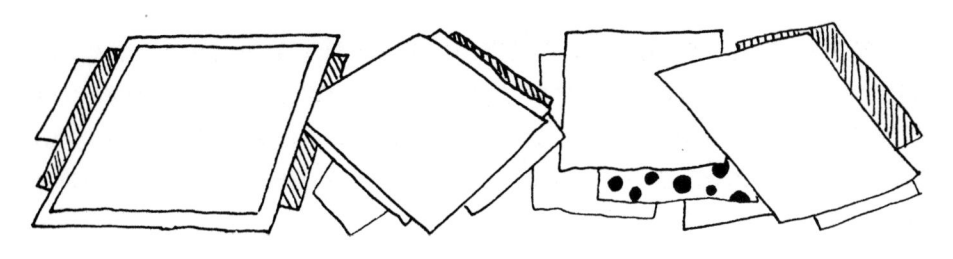

CHOOSING YOUR PAPER

Paper comes in different textures, weights, sizes and colors. The kind of paper you use depends on two things: (1) are you making a card or poster and (2) what kind of technique are you using. For most posters, you will want to use a heavy paper, so that it will not tear or rip. For cards, you will either want to use stiff cardboard (for postcard style greeting cards) or lightweight paper (for French-folded cards). Check the technique that you want to use to make sure that your paper is appropriate. You can have a lot of fun folding paper for both greeting cards and posters. Sometimes when you are using heavy paper, you will need to score it before you fold it.

you need: ruler, mat knife or scissors, pencil and a newspaper (to protect your working surface).

Using the ruler as a guide, draw the pencil line where you want to fold the paper. Then, again using the ruler as a guide, draw one blade of the scissors or the mat knife along the line. Then it will be easy to fold a straight line along the scoring.

ARRANGING YOUR LETTERING

Lettering comes in two basic types: block letters or print, and script letters. On a card, your letters should not overpower your artwork. In a poster, the letters should be outstanding, and there should be enough space around each word and letter so that it can be read easily from a distance.

Script letters go well with gentle curvy artwork, while block letters go well with strong, angular pictures. When you letter your card or poster, you may want to draw very light lines with your ruler to make sure that your letter doesn't go downhill, and is even. Some people sketch in the letters in pencil first, and then go over them. If you do this, make sure that the letters are very light, so they don't show through.

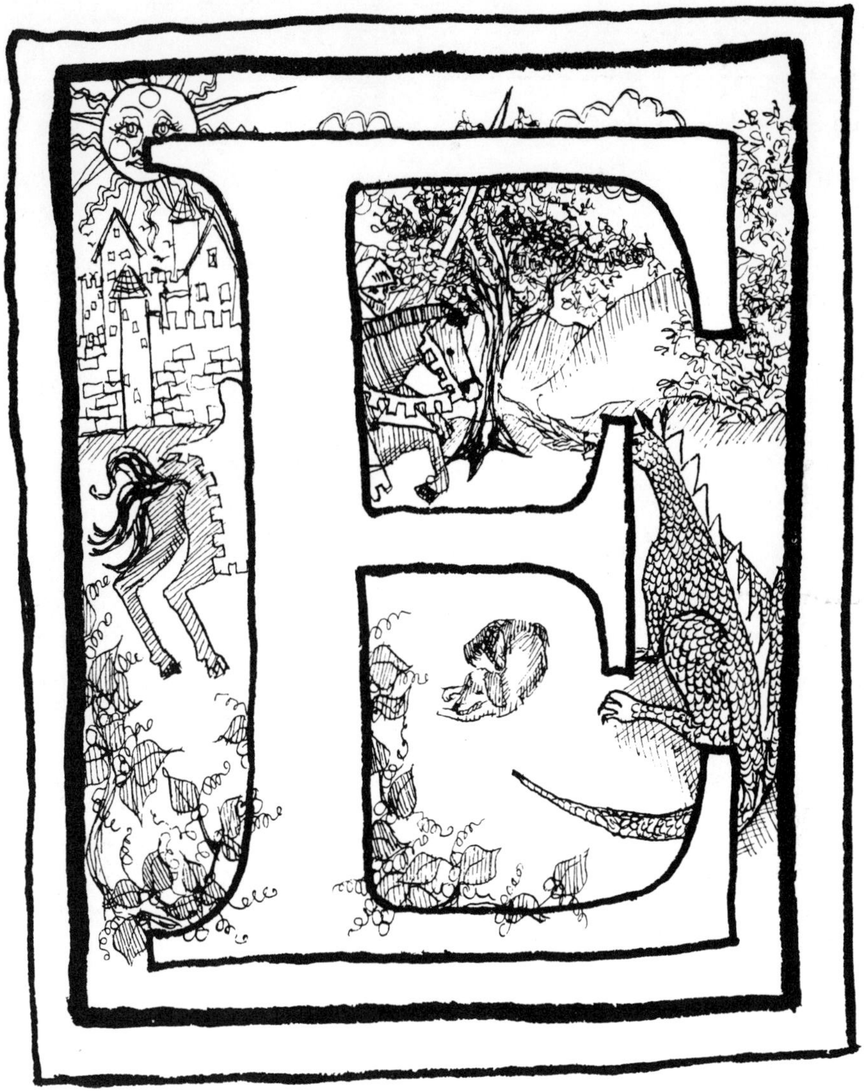

What bus crosses the ocean?

happy COLUMBUS day!

IV HOW TO DO IT: ONE AT A TIME

CRAYON TECHNIQUES

CRAYONS AND OIL PASTELS

There are two kinds of crayons: wax crayons, which you've probably been using since before you could talk, and oil crayons, sometimes called oil pastels. When you draw with crayons, be sure to cover your working surface with newspapers. This protects the table, and gives you a softer surface so that your crayons draw more smoothly. For strong lines, use the point of the crayon. You can hit the point of the crayon sharply against the paper to make freckles of color: this is called stippling. For softer shading, use the side of the crayon, rubbing it gently across your paper.

SCRATCHBOARD

You need: oil pastels
table knife or nail
newspaper
cardboard
wax crayons

First, spread the newspaper on the table because scratchboard is a surprisingly messy technique. Choose a color from your wax crayons and cover the entire cardboard with it. Press down fairly hard, coloring first from left to right and then up and down. Now choose one of your oil pastels and crayon over the first color with this.

You can build up several oil-pastel layers, but remember that crayon tends to flake off as you add layer on layer, and the oil pastel may smear.

Scratch a drawing on the crayon-covered cardboard with the edge of a table knife or the tip of a nail. You will see the colors underneath—the harder you press, the more layers of color will show through.

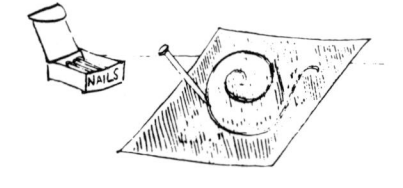

If you want to have a lot of different colors, you can make your bottom layer of crayon in stripes or smaller areas of several colors. Remember to use the color that you want for the background last as the top layer.

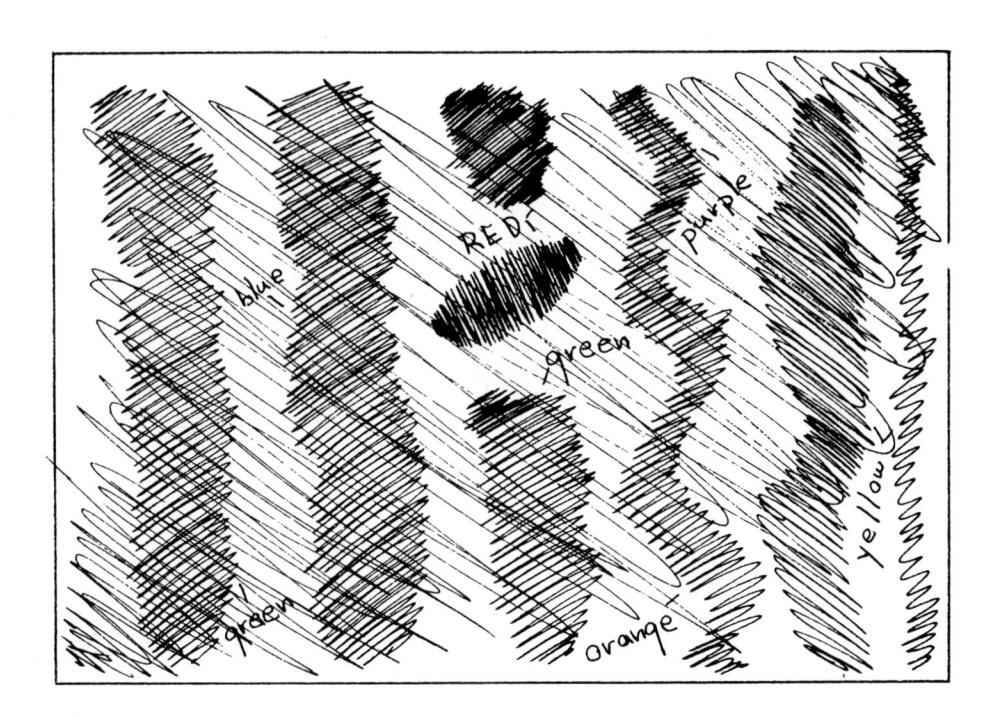

My name is Zero.
I'm lost
REWARD
If you find me,
please return
me to Stephen,
ApT. 2-C.

PAINT TECHNIQUES

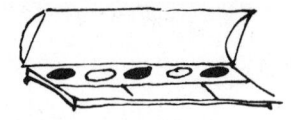

WATERCOLORS AND POSTER PAINTS

Watercolor and poster paints don't require a lot of special preparation and equipment. By varying the amount of water you add to the paint, you can paint a dark blue car and a pale blue sky with the same jar of paint, by using no water for the dark blue, and adding a lot of water for the light blue. A good selection of paint brushes might include a number 4, a number 8, a number 11. Using varying amounts of the brush you can vary the widths of your strokes. To get the feel of your brushes, practice ahead of time on a piece of scrap paper.

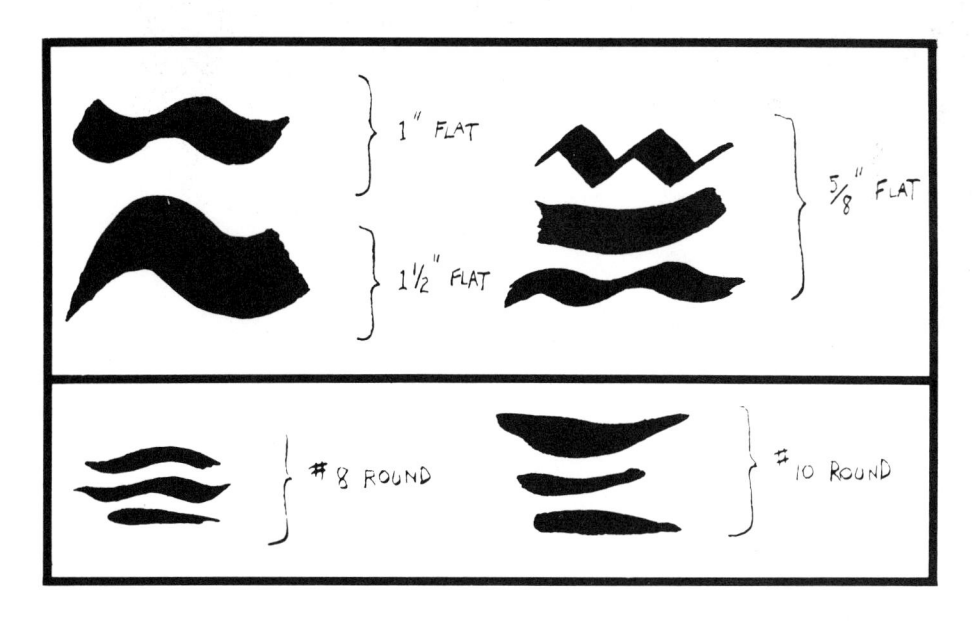

You need: jar of tepid water (change it often!)
a sponge
brushes
watercolor or poster paint
heavy, rough-textured paper

There are all sorts of things that you can do with watercolor or poster paint: You can cover a whole sheet of paper with color using a sponge or large brush; this is called a wash. Or you can stipple with a small brush, hitting the paper lightly with the tip of the brush, as shown in the picture.

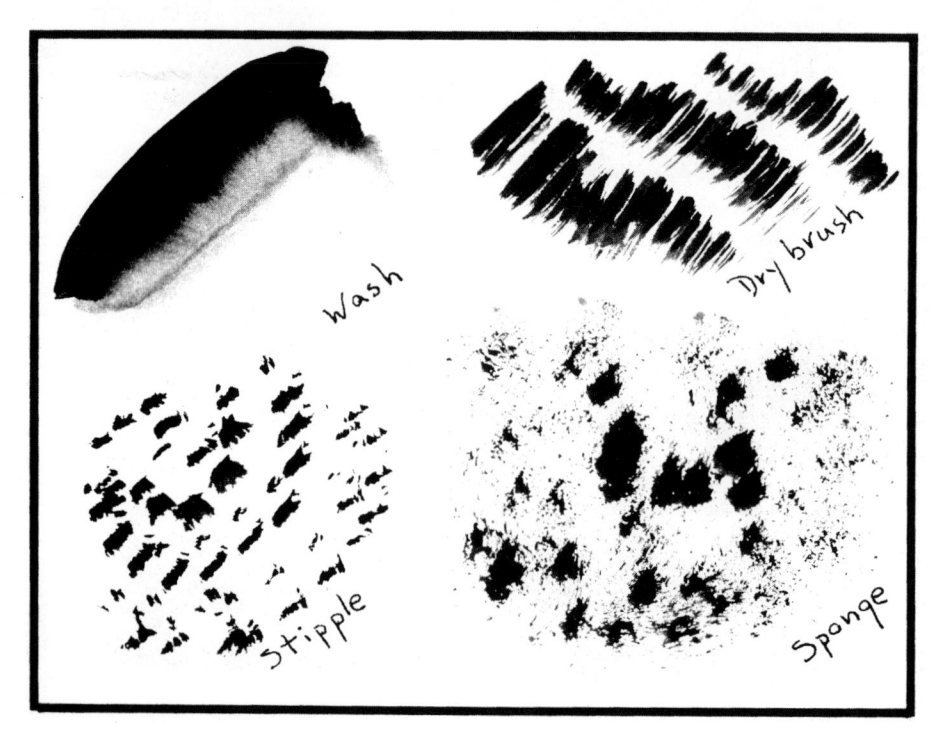

To produce another interesting watercolor effect, paint on only one side of the paper. While the paint is still wet, fold the paper in half. The design transfers to the other side. This is very effective for abstract designs.

INK OR FOOD COLOR PAINTING

You need: drinking straw
               paper
               different colors of food color or ink

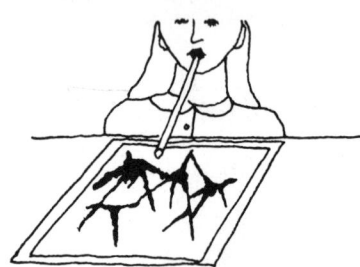

Cover your working surface with newspaper.

Put several puddles (no bigger than a penny) of ink on the paper.

Place your straw close to the puddle, but not actually in it. Gently blow the ink across the paper.

Then move to the next puddle. By controlling how you blow, you can make interesting patterns.

TEMPERA RESIST

This process is called resist or batik. Using the principle that water and wax don't mix, the paint, which is watery, and the crayon, which is waxy, fill up different areas of the picture for interesting effects.

You need: tempera (or watercolors)
crayons
brushes
newspaper
heavy, rough-textured paper

Draw a simple design with your crayons, leaving a lot of open space. Press heavily on the crayons so that the wax is evenly distributed.

Now paint in the empty spaces. You will notice that the paint rolls off the areas where the crayon is. Keep the paints watery so that you can see the difference in texture between the paint and the crayon.

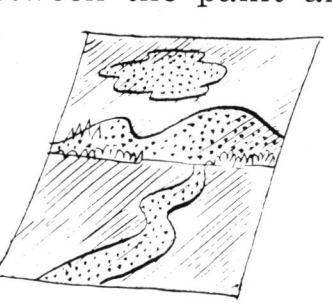

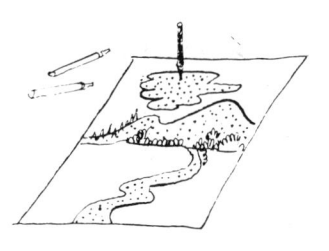

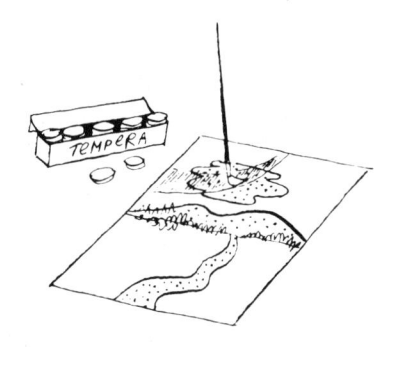

PASTEL PAINTS

Don't throw out your old bits of worn-down pastels. Here's a way to recycle them by converting them into paint.

You need: turpentine
newspaper
glass jars with lids
extra lids
brushes
smooth, hard-finish paper
oil pastels

Spread newspaper on your working surface.

Peel the paper off the pastels. Put each color in a separate glass jar with turpentine —if you mix colors, you will come out with dull brown paint. Screw the lid on each jar tightly, and wait about two hours. When you take off the lid, you will see paint!

The colors will be the same as your original pastels, and now you can mix them to make new colors. For example, yellow mixed with blue makes green, red mixed with blue makes purple, and red mixed with yellow gives you orange. Mix the colors a little bit at a time in your spare lids.

You can use these oil-base paints the same way you do watercolors (See page 54 for information about brush strokes.), but you can't dilute them with water, or wash your brush with water. You must use turpentine, or another oil solvent, such as linseed oil. After you have finished painting, soak your brushes in turpentine and then wash them with soap and warm water so they will not dry out.

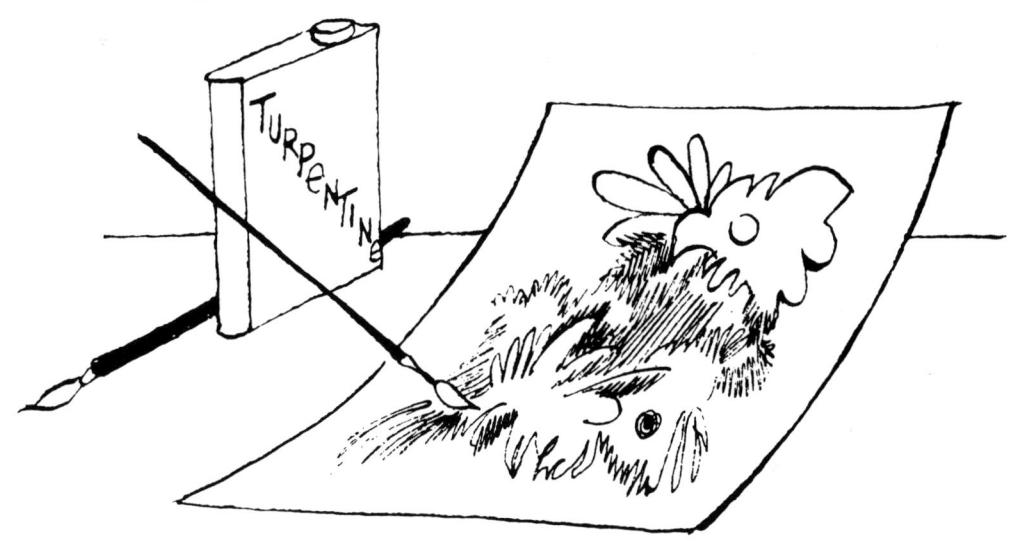

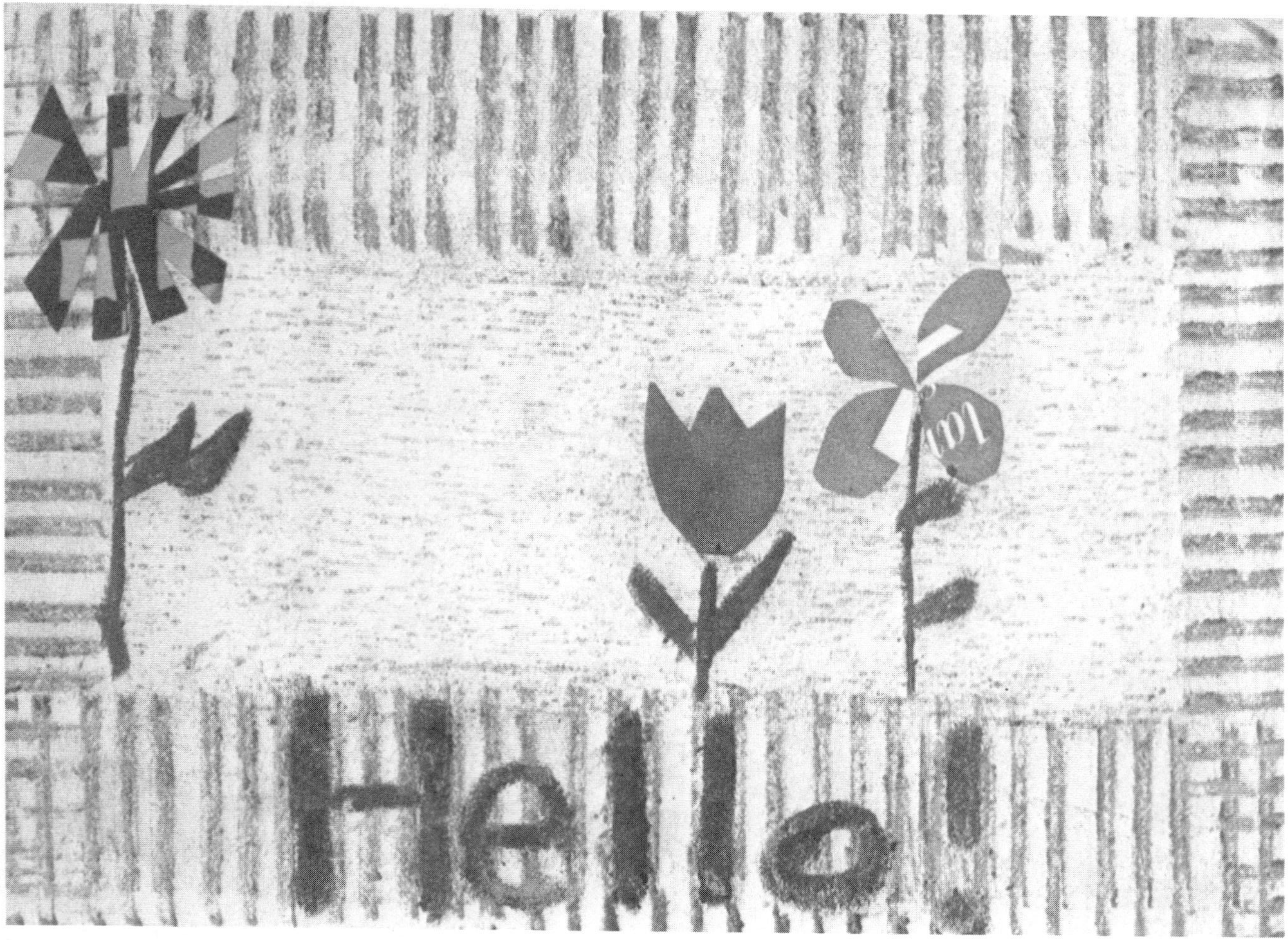
Hello!

TRANSFER TECHNIQUES
OFFSET TRACINGS

Sometimes you see a design or a picture that you'd like to copy for your card. Here's how:

You need: tracing paper
number 1 pencil
watercolors and brushes, crayons or magic markers
masking tape
spoon

Select a picture to copy. It can be one of your own designs or a book or magazine illustration.

Place a sheet of tracing paper over the design, and secure it with masking tape.

Check to see that your pencil is sharp. If it isn't, sharpen it.

Outline the picture with your pencil. Remove the tracing paper, pulling the tape up carefully so that it doesn't rip the page you've used.

Turn the tracing paper over and go over your lines on the under side.

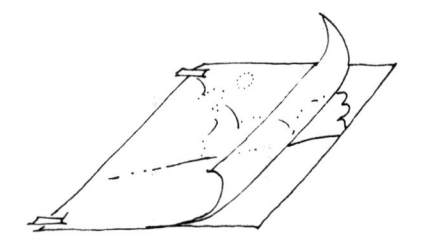

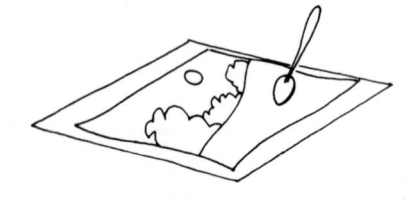

Put the tracing paper on the sheet of paper you are going to use for your greeting card, with the top side down. Rub your tracing with the back of a spoon.

You can expect to print about four copies. If you want to make more, go over the drawing again on both sides of the paper with your pencil. Repeat this as many times as you need to.

Your copies will turn out soft and subdued compared to the original. You can go over the lines with magic marker or crayon, and you can color in the picture with watercolors or crayon to give it the look you like.

RUBBINGS

Rubbing is a transfer technique from patterned surfaces. What can you use for rubbings? Cinder blocks, concrete sidewalk, bricks, cork, the stamped front covers of books, bamboo place mats, combs, and coins are just some of the interesting textures you can recreate on paper.

You need: wax crayons or oil pastels
            lightweight, sturdy paper

For delicate patterns, like the pattern on a coin, sharpen crayon. For rougher patterns that are more defined, you will want to use crayon or pastel.

Spread your paper over the surface you want to use for your rubbing.

If it is a large flat surface, like a concrete sidewalk, run your crayon with the long side down lightly across the paper. If it is not dark enough, go over the paper a second time.

If it is a small surface—like a coin—use the sharpened tip of your crayon to go over the surface.

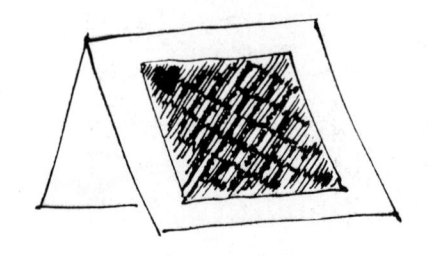

Now look at your paper. Is the pattern even? If not, you will want to touch up the places that are blurry. With a coin rubbing, you might want to go over the outline with a sharp crayon.

If you use a surface with an interesting texture but no design, you can draw a crayon picture over it.

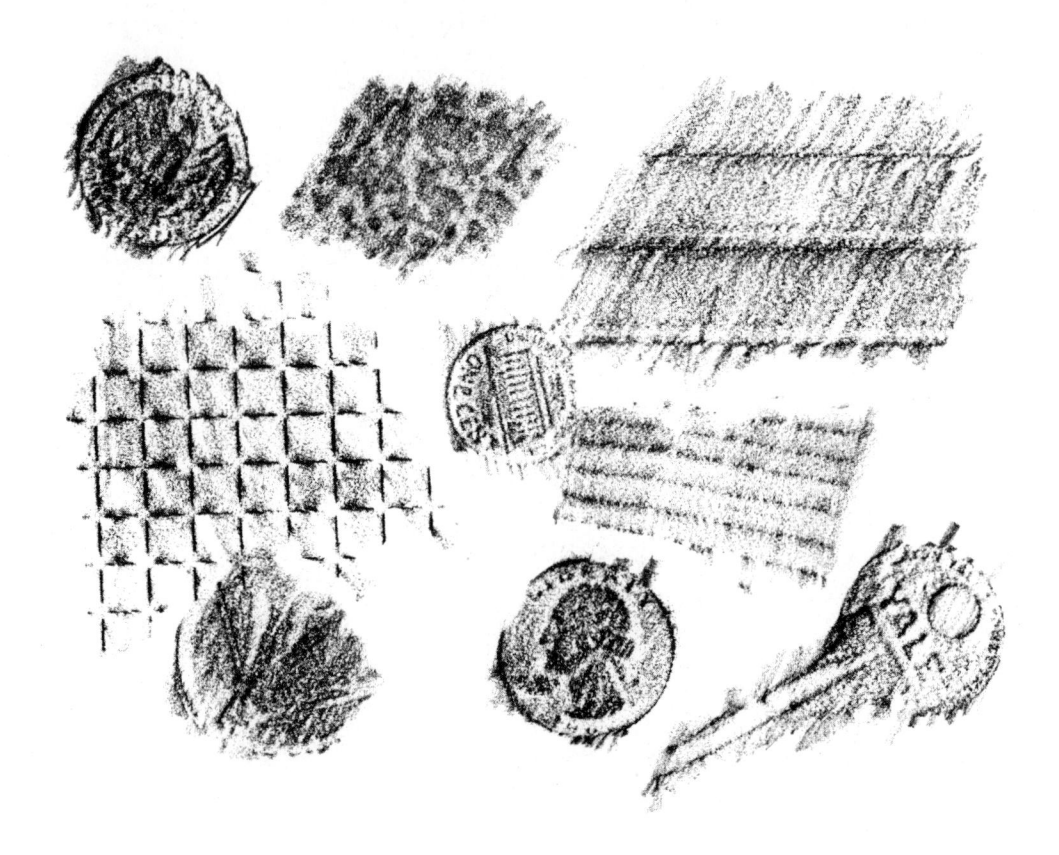

MONOPRINT

A monoprint is a design painted on glass or plastic and then transferred to paper. Monoprint literally means "single print," and no two are exactly alike. But it's easy to change or renew your design by wiping off the surface with a sponge and starting again.

You need: a smooth piece of glass or plastic
              tempera paint   spoon
              ink roller   toothpicks
              paint brushes mirror

   Paint a design on the glass (or plastic), or cover the surface with paint and scratch in a picture or design with toothpicks.

   Place a sheet of paper on the glass over the wet paint. Smooth the paper down with the heel of your hands. When the sheet is flat, rub it a few times with a spoon.

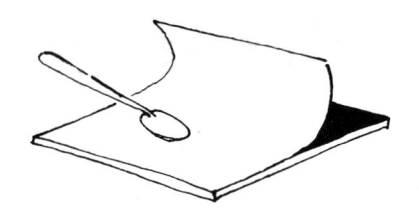

Lift the paper up at two corners and grasp the edges. Gently but quickly lift it off the glass.

Now you are ready to make another monoprint. Wipe off your first print with water, and put down a new layer of paint. Remember that your design will print in reverse, so you will want to check with a mirror, especially if you include lettering.

CARD SALE

Proceeds To Troop 181
Eaton School

2¢   To $1.00

TODAY   in the GYM

HAPPY FATHER'S DAY

TO A DAD WHO WORKS

AND SLEEPS

AND WORKS

COLLAGE TECHNIQUES
COLLAGE

Collage is the art of pasting materials onto a stiff sheet of paper to make an interesting design or a picture. We will show you three basic styles of collage, and you can develop your own ideas from there.

The effect you achieve depends on the kind of matrial you choose. Any thin, small object can be used on a collage greeting card, but remember that if you are going to send a collage card through the mail it shouldn't be too fragile.

One of the best things about collage is that you can find materials everywhere. If your mother sews, ask her to put aside odd buttons and little scraps of cloth for your collage collection. Some people keep a large envelope of collage material they come across to use for making cards. You can collect snippets of paper from cutting up other cards, twigs and leaves from outdoors, small seashells from the beach, and string from packages.

Collage of Materials
You need: Colored scraps of paper, fabric, wallpaper, felt, yarn, ribbons, sequins
White glue or rubber cement
Gummed colored paper

Here's a good project using this technique. Make your own substitutions for the suggested materials—that's what collage is all about.

Cut a round piece of felt for the face. Paste this on a stiff sheet of paper. Paste two small buttons or sequins onto felt for the eyes. Cut out a triangular piece of construction paper for the nose and a round piece for the mouth. Use pieces of yarn for the hair and eyebrows. Cut out of fabric a triangular piece for the dress. From pieces of wallpaper make the arms and and legs. Paste pistachio nut shells for the hands and finish off with flat pieces of macaroni for the feet.

Glitter Collage

You need: glitter
stiff paper
white glue
small stiff brush
cardboard box (shoe box works well)
pen or pencil

Make a card design on a piece of stiff paper. Complete it (including the message on the reverse side), leaving blank the area you want to cover with glitter.

Brush on glue evenly within the blank area.

Put your card face up in the cardboard box.

Sprinkle the glitter over the glued area.

Shake the card back and forth to distribute the glitter evenly.

Reuse glitter that falls off.

String Collage

    You need: string or colored yarn
                             white glue
                             stiff paper
                             pen or pencil

Make a simple line drawing in pencil on your card. This will be your string line.

Fill in the lettering and borders until the card is all finished except for the string picture.

Spread white glue neatly along the outlines of your drawing.

Quickly, before the glue dries, press string on colored yarn along the lines of your string picture.

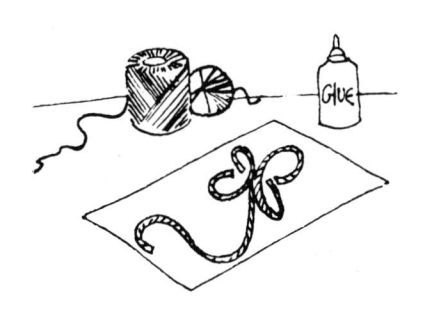

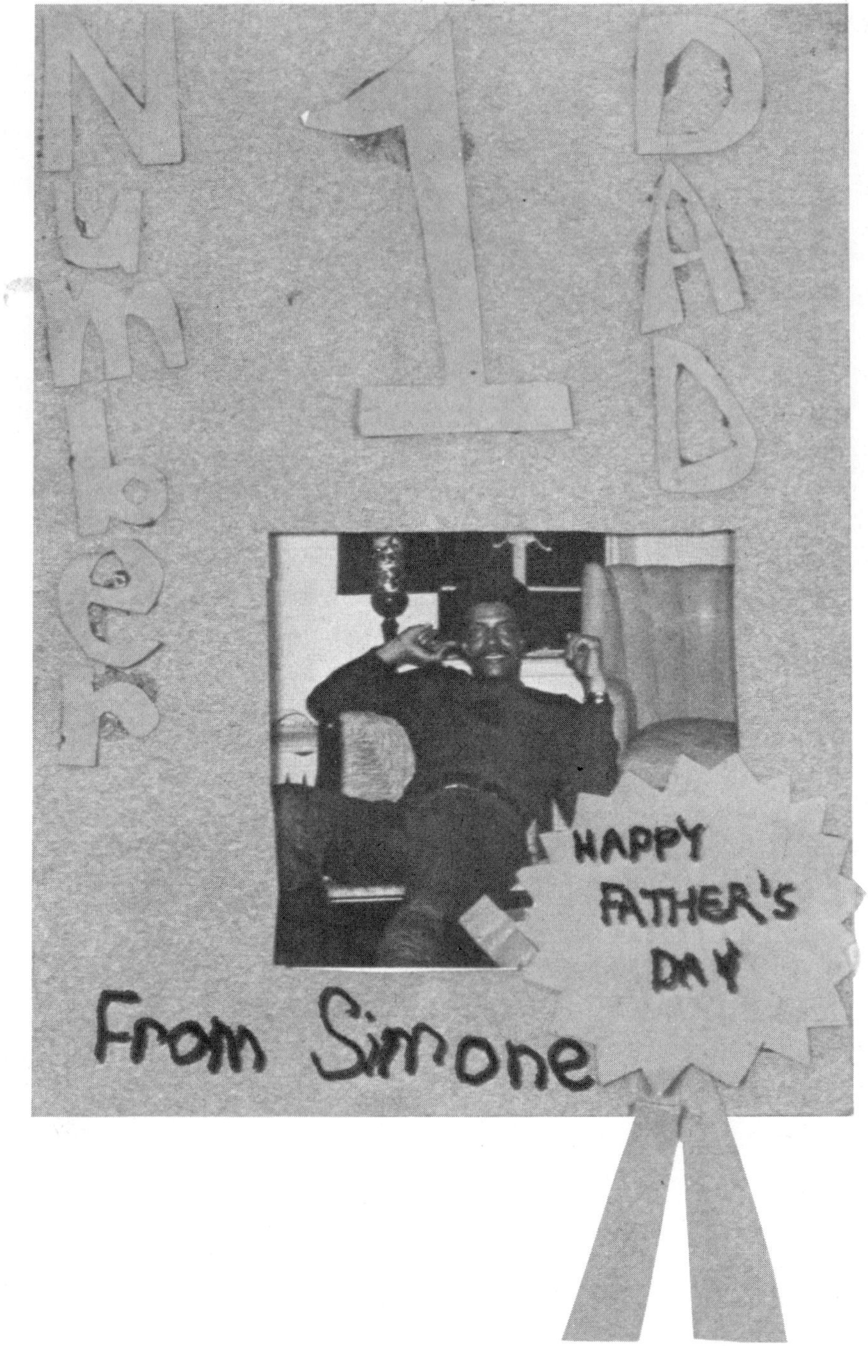
Number 1 DAD
HAPPY FATHER'S DAY
From Simone

MOUNTING TECHNIQUES

INSERT METHOD

The insert method works well for art drawn on heavy paper, or for photographs.

You need: matte knife or scissors
heavy paper (construction paper)
rubber cement with brush
ruler

Fold your cardboard in half, or your construction paper in a French-fold, by first folding it in half lengthwise, then folding it in half crosswise.

Measure your artwork. Decide how much of it you want to be visible on the front of the card. Place your French-folded card so the uncut edges are at the left and top. Transfer the measurements of your artwork to the card with a light pencil line.

Now cut inside the line to make a hole. Unfold the card and brush rubber cement around the cut area.

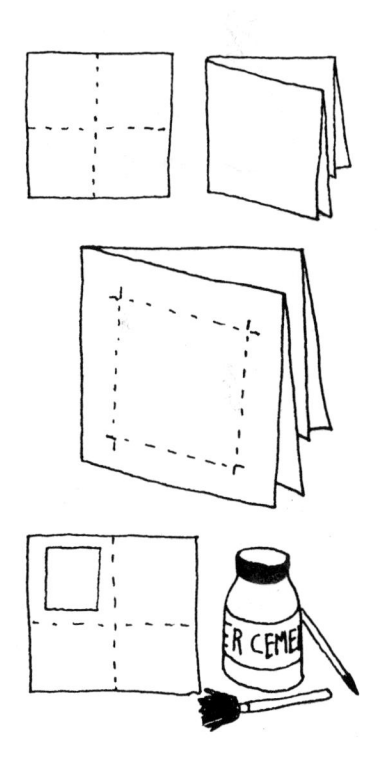

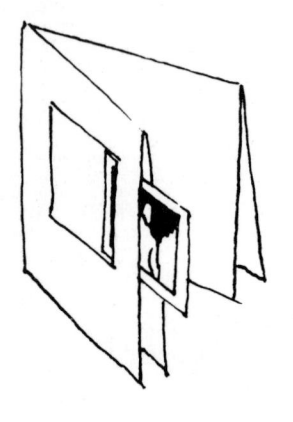

Then brush rubber cement along the edges of your artwork.

When it is tacky, place your insert face up so that the glued surfaces lie together. Press the glued edges with your ruler.

Refold the card. Put some rubber cement along the edges between page one and page two and seal in your picture.

If you have several small pictures, you can make several holes to frame each one.

TOP MOUNTING

Top mounting works well if you are making a postcard greeting card. Your card should be made of cardboard for best results from this technique. In this method, the artwork goes directly on the front of the card.

You need: pencil
                stiff cardboard
                rubber cement with brush
                ruler
                metallic paper (optional)
                rick rack (optional)
                paint (optional)

Measure your picture. Allow good sized margins, and space for lettering, using your dummy as a guide. You may want to paint the cardboard, or paste a piece of colorful paper as a background.

Now spread rubber cement on the back of the picture. Cut a piece of cardboard large enough to leave room for margins and lettering. Trace off the area needed for picture with light pencil marks and brush on cement.

Wait a few seconds until rubber cement gets tacky and place on marked-off area of card. For a variation, you might frame the picture with strips of metallic paper or rickrack. Or you can paint a frame around your picture.

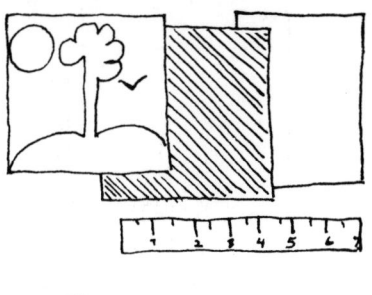

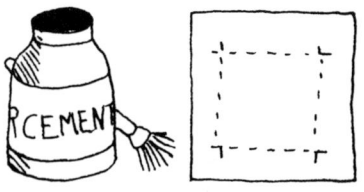

TUESDAY, DECEMBER 22
AT 3:45 IN THE AUDITORIUM

Christmas Concert

V
HOW TO DO IT: MAKING MULTIPLES

PRINTING TECHNIQUES

LINOLEUM BLOCK PRINTING

Linoleum printing is one of the easiest ways to make many copies of a simple design. You can print a single design in many colors.

You need: linoleum in 3" x 5" pieces (use ¼" thick battleship linoleum)
tempera colors
linoleum knives
brushes   sponge
mirror
scratch paper and soft pencil
carbon paper (optional)
pencil
pie tin

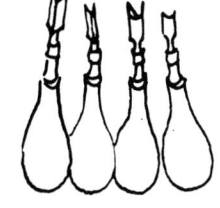

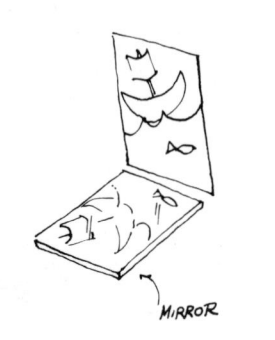

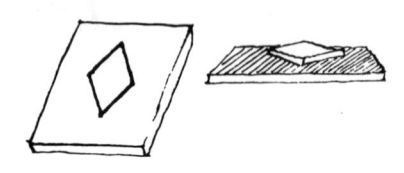

If you've never made linoleum prints before, practice handling your cutting tools.

Work out your design on scratch paper. Once you have a good idea of what you want, draw directly on the linoleum. Your sketch will be reversed when printed, so look at it in a mirror before you actually start to cut.

Draw your design. Cut around your design, keeping in mind that only the raised parts will print.

Sponge on tempera paint evenly on the raised areas. Place your block on the already folded card to print. Hold it in place a few seconds before raising it, and when you do raise it, raise it straight to avoid smudging.

You can wash off your linoleum blocks and use them many times with different colors of inks.

STAMPED PRINTS

You need: any firm-fleshed vegetable or fruit
knife (fairly sharp with a short blade)
tempera paint   newspaper
heavy, porous paper
scratch paper   pencil

Cover your working surface with newspaper. Cut the vegetable so there's enough of it to hold onto, and the widest possible flat surface for making your design.

Trace the size of your vegetable surface, and draw a design within that area on a piece of scratch paper. Hold a mirror to it, and adjust your design so that when it is reversed in printing it is the way you want it.

With a sharp pencil, draw a design on the vegetable surface. Press hard enough so that you break the surface.

Carve out the surface you don't want to print.

Dip your "stamp" into a saucer filled with tempera paint. Press on your paper, folded to the size you want your card.

Repeat. You can rinse the tempera paint off and change colors, but the vegetable will not last more than one day.

COME TO OUR Halloween Party

3 O'CLOCK
HYDE Playground
Weds. Oct. 31
PRIZES

STENCIL TECHNIQUES
STENCILS

You need: small stiff-bristled brush
heavy paper or cardboard
scissors
spray or poster paints, crayons, magic markers

To make your stencil, cut shapes or letters into a piece of heavy paper, or cardboard.

Place the cardboard over your greeting card paper and hold it firmly.

With a stiff brush, apply paint through the cut openings to the paper underneath. You can also use spray or poster paint, crayons, or magic marker.

Always color from the top of the stencil towards the center. This will prevent the paint from slipping under the edges of the stencil.

By repeating the process in different parts of the card, you can create a pattern.

SILK SCREEN

Silk screen is one of the oldest methods of making many copies of one design. It was used thousands of years ago in China. Basically, it is a stencil process in which colored inks are squeezed through the openings in a piece of cloth.

Complete silk-screen sets can be bought in stores, ranging from small ones for beginners for about $9.00 apiece, to large ones which can cost about $25.00, including paints and directions. However, it's easy enough to put together your own silk screen set. Here's how:

You need: picture frame   hammer or stapler
piece of silk or nylon net, 1" wider on all sides than the picture frame
carpet tacks or staples

Remove the glass from the picture frame. Remove all the tacks in the picture frame. Save the glass for making monoprints.

Stretch the cloth tightly across the frame. Attach it with carpet tacks or staples.

Check to make sure that the material is taut in all directions.

This is your silk-screen frame. Here is a way to print colored shapes on a white background.

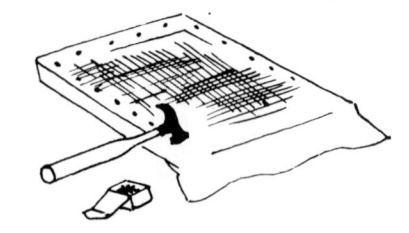

You need: scratch paper and pencil
glue, clear nail polish or shellac
masking tape
brush
flexible, heavy paper
paint
cardboard
newspaper
brown paper
scissors
silk-screen frame

Make a preliminary sketch of the picture you want to print. When it satisfies you, draw it on heavy brown paper (a cut-up bag is fine) and then cut it out. After a little practice, you'll see that the simpler your shapes, the more effective they are.

Tape masking tape around the edges of your silk-screen frame. Now seal with tape the edges of the frame on the inside as well.

Cover your working surface with newspaper. Turn the picture frame so that the outside is lying on the newspaper. Place your shapes on the frame. With clear nail polish or shellac, brush over them, particularly around the edges. This holds them in place.

Place the paper you want to use for your card under the screen.

Put some colored paint along the inside edge of the screen. With a heavy, stiff piece of cardboard, firmly and evenly spread the paint across the frame.

Lift up the screen slowly from the paper and remove the print. Avoid too much delay between prints, as your color may dry on the screen. Your finished print should be clear and sharp. White specks mean that you are applying too little pressure as you spread the paint, or that your paint is too dry.

VI
THAT EXTRA BONUS

As you make more and more greeting cards, and posters, you'll find that you're better at it; you know what works and what doesn't and the ideas will come more easily. People may say to you, "I loved your Christmas card, I wish I could buy some like it," or "What a great poster—you should sell it!"

You *can* make greeting cards and posters to sell. Since most people can't afford to pay you for the time it takes to make a single watercolor poster or a fancy collage card, you will most likely want to make multiple copies using stencil and printing techniques (see Chapter V). If you have some money to invest in this project, you can make one basic design in black ink and have it xeroxed, printed, or mimeographed. Then you can color in the designs. One hundred years ago, most cards were made this way.

A large group like a school or a camp can sponsor a contest for the best greeting card or poster. In New York City, the Little Red Schoolhouse and St. Hilda's and St. Hugh's School have annual contests and the first-prize card is then printed professionally and sold to raise funds for the school. The American Legion sponsors an annual poppy poster contest. For information you can write to:

> American Legion Auxiliary
> National Headquarters
> 777 North Meridian Street
> Indianapolis, Indiana 46204

This contest closes on March first of each year, and offers 3 $100 prizes.

If you enjoy making greeting cards and posters you may want to consider it as a career.

VII
MAILING CARDS AND POSTING POSTERS

The Post Office will not send any letter that is smaller than 3″ x 4¼″. If you want to send a large poster, your best bet is to roll it carefully and put it in a mailing tube. Mailing tubes are available at stationary stores and many dime stores. If you want to mail a tiny card, put it in a slightly larger envelope that meets the post office regulations. You can cut cardboard to keep the card from being crushed. Or, if you have a fancy card, you can mark your envelope, "Hand Cancel". For odd-shaped cards, you can make your own envelope following the suggestions pictured on page 89.

When you post a poster, you are best off with masking tape. Masking tape sticks to most surfaces without hurting them, and you can peel it off your poster without disturbing your artwork. If you are posting your poster on a bulletin board, use tacks or push pins but don't push them through your poster. Press them along its edges, as shown in the picture.

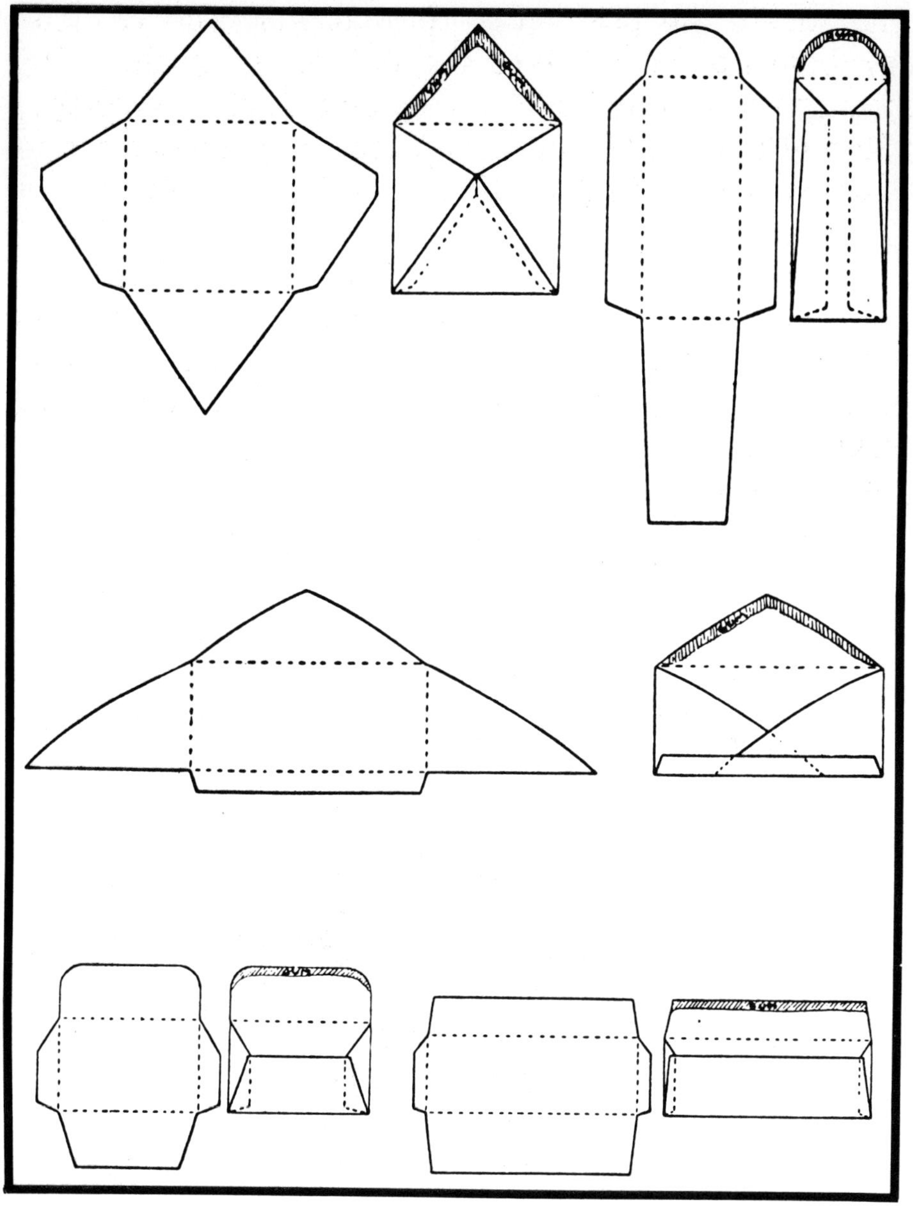

VIII
WHERE TO FIND SUPPLIES

One of the best things about making posters and greeting cards is that you can easily find materials around the house. Cereal, pantyhose, and shirts all come with lightweight cardboard that is just right for making greeting cards. Old magazines are gold mines of colorful pictures for collages. Brown paper bags can be cut up for scratch paper or as an interesting background for a poster. Wrapping paper and wallpaper scraps often get tossed away—why not save them to use in your posters and greeting cards?

When materials are scarce at home, there are a number of free sources for art supplies. If you know someone who sews, ask her to save scraps of cloth, rickrack and edging for you. Travel agencies, airlines and service stations all offer maps and colorful brochures free for the asking. These can be used effectively in making posters and greeting cards too.

Your local dime store is a good supply center for glitter, basic papers, crayons, paints, and pencils. For more sophisticated supplies, you should check an art supply store. If there are none in your area, you can write to these firms for mail-order catalogs of art supplies:

> A. I. Friedman
> 25 West 45th Street
> New York, N.Y. 10036

> Arthur Brown and Company
> 2 West 46th Street
> New York, N.Y. 10036

Lettering sets, including drawing and lettering pens with special nibs, can be ordered from:

> Visual Art Industries
> 68 Thirty-third Street
> Brooklyn, N.Y. 11232

For special collage material, you can write to these places for old pictures and scraps:

> Brandon Memorabilia
> 3 West 30th Street
> New York, N.Y. 10001

For gummed paper:

> Jo Ann Imports
> 4436 West Slauson Street
> Los Angeles, California

For sequins and glitter:
    Holiday Handicrafts
    10 Bridge Street
    Winstead, Connecticut 06098

    Dennison Manufacturing Company
    370 Lexington Avenue
    New York, N.Y. 10017

    International Assemblix
    P. O. Box 878
    Toledo, Ohio 43601

BIBLIOGRAPHY

TECHNIQUES

Alkema, Chester. *Complete Crayon Book.* New York: Sterling, 1969.

Carlis, John. *How To Make Your Own Greeting Cards.* New York: Watson Guptill, 1968.

Hart, Tony. *The Young Letterer: A How It's Done Book of Lettering.* New York: Warne, 1966.

Horn, George. *Posters.* Worcester, Massachusetts: Davis Maas, 1964.

Kohn, Eugene. *Photography: A Manual for Shutterbugs.* Englewood Cliffs, New Jersey: Prentice-Hall, 1965.

Leeming, Joseph. *Fun With Greeting Cards.* Philadelphia: Lippincott, 1960.

Marks, Mickey. *Collage.* New York: Dial, 1968.

Purdy, Susan. *Holiday Cards for You to Make.* Philadelphia: Lippincott, 1967.

Rachow, Leo. *Postercraft*. New York: Sterling, 1969.

Rainey, Sarita and Burton Wasserman. *Basic Silkscreen Printmaking*. Worcester, Massachusetts: Davis Maas, 1970.

Seidleman, James and Grace Minoyne. *Creating With Paint*. New York: Crowell-Collier, 1967.

Weiss, Harvey. *Paper, Ink and Roller*. Reading, Massachusetts: Young Scott, (Addison-Wesley), 1967.

———. *Pen, Pencil and Brush*. Reading, Massachusetts: Young Scott, (Addison-Wesley), 1967.

Zaidenberg, Arthur. *How To Paint With Watercolors*. New York: Vanguard, 1968.

GENERAL

Chase, Ernest. *Romance of Greeting Cards*. Detroit: Gale, 1926, reprinted 1967.

Cirker, Hayward and Blanche. *Golden Age of the Poster*. New York: Dover, 1972.

Hiller, Bevis. *100 Years of Posters*. New York: Harper, 1972.

McSpadden, J. Walker. *Book of Holidays*. New York: Crowell, 1968.

Secrist, Elizabeth. *Red-Letter Days*. Philadelphia: Macrae, 1965.

INDEX

American Legion
   Poster Contest   86
Anniversaries   22
Art Supplies   90
Bake Sale Poster   30
Bar Mitzvah   21
Bas Mitzvah   21
Batik   57
Beardsley, Aubrey   8
Birthday Cards   38
Birthday Poster   41
Bon Voyage Cards   26
Book Fair Poster   33
Brush Techniques   45
Charity Poster   37
Christmas   13, 34, 37
Class Election Poster   14
Class Play Poster   17
Collage   69
   Glitter   70
   Material   91
   String   71
Columbus Day   30
Confirmation   21
Congratulations   26
Contests, Poster   86
Crayon   49
Dummy   42

Easter   18
Engagement   22
Envelopes   89
Father's Day   22
Friendship Cards   18
Folding
Food Color Painting   56
Get Well Cards   13
Glitter   70, 92
Graduation   21
Greenaway, Kate   8
Groundhog Day   14
Halloween   30
Hanukkah   36
Hebrew New Year   28
Invitations   40
Lemonade Sale Poster   25
Lincoln, Abraham   33
Lettering   46, 91
Linoleum Block   77
Lost Pet Poster   18
Monoprint   65
Mother's Day   21
Mounting   73
   Insert   73
   Top   74
New Apartment or
   Home   25

New Year 13
No Litter Poster 22
Nutrition Poster 28
Offset Tracings 61
Oil Pastels 49
Parrish, Maxfield 10
Paper 45
Parade Poster 21
Park Program Poster 26
Passover 18
Pastel Paints 58
Plays, Announcement 17
    Program 17
Poster Paints 53
Poppy Poster Contest 86
Post Office 87
Prang, Louis 8
Recycling Poster 25
Register Your Bike
    Poster 18
Rubbings 63
Saint Patrick 17
Santa Claus 34
Scout Meeting Poster 28
Scratchboard 50
Shahn, Ben 10
Silk Screen 82
Snow Safety Poster 13
Stamped Prints 78
Stencil 81

String Collage 71
Stippling 49, 54
Supplies
    Where to find 90
Sympathy Cards 33
Team Recruitment
    Poster 14
Tempera Resist 57
Thanksgiving 33
Thank You Cards 39
Tooth Poster 30
Toulouse-Lautrec,
    Henri de 8
Valentine Day 3, 14
Watercolor 53
Wedding 22
Yom Kippur 29